D1060447

HISTORY'S GREATEST RIVALS

ELIZABETH I OF ENGLAND Vs. MARY, QUEEN OF SCOTS

BATTLE FOR THE THRONE

Ellis Roxburgh

Gareth Stevens
PUBLISHING

Please visit our website, **www.garethstevens.com**.
For a free color catalog of all our high-quality books,
call toll free 1-800-542-2595 or fax 1-877-542-2596.

Library of Congress Cataloging-in-Publication Data

Roxburgh, Ellis.
  Elizabeth I of England vs. Mary, Queen of Scots : battle for the throne / Ellis Roxburgh.
    pages cm — (History's greatest rivals)
  Includes index.
  ISBN 978-1-4824-4227-4 (pbk.)
  ISBN 978-1-4824-4228-1 (6 pack)
  ISBN 978-1-4824-4229-8 (library binding)
  1. Elizabeth I, Queen of England, 1533-1603—Juvenile literature. 2. Mary, Queen of Scots,
1542-1587—Juvenile literature. 3. Great Britain—History—Elizabeth, 1558-1603—Juvenile
literature. 4. Scotland—History—Mary Stuart, 1542-1567—Juvenile literature. 5. Great
Britain—Kings and rulers—Succession—History—16th century—Juvenile literature. I. Title.
  DA355.R69 2016
  941.05'50922—dc23

                            2015021629

Published in 2016 by
Gareth Stevens Publishing
111 East 14th Street, Suite 349
New York, NY 10003

Copyright © 2016 Brown Bear Books Ltd

For Brown Bear Books Ltd:
Editorial Director: Lindsey Lowe
Managing Editor: Tim Cooke
Children's Publisher: Anne O'Daly
Design Manager: Keith Davis
Designer: Lynne Lennon
Picture Manager: Sophie Mortimer

Picture Credits: T=Top, C=Center, B=Bottom, L=Left, R=Right. Front Cover: National Portrait
Gallery: r; Robert Hunt Library: l; Shutterstock: Steve Estvanik background. Bridgeman
Art Library: 20; istockphoto: 16; National Archives: 33; National Galleries of Scotland: 19;
National Portrait Gallery: 13, 25, 30, 31; Philip Mould Gallery: 1; Prado Museum: 36; Robert
Hunt Library: 7, 10, 17, 24, 39, 40; Royal Collection: 18; Scottish National Gallery: 11; Senate
House Library: 21; Shutterstock: 27, 32, George Kollidas 9, Alexandra Reinwald 6; Tate: 29;
Thinkstock: Tony Baggett 14, Dave Head 28, Photos.com 8, 15, 22, 23, 37, 41, Songdquan
Deng 12; Topfoto: British Library Boart 34, The Granger Collection 26, 35; Kim Traynor: 38.

Brown Bear Books has made every attempt to contact the copyright holder. If anyone
has any information please contact licensing@brownbearbooks.co.uk

Manufactured in the United States of America

CPSIA compliance information: Batch #CW16GS. For further information contact
Gareth Stevens, New York, New York at 1-800-542-2595.

CONTENTS

At Odds 4

Context 6

Lines Are Drawn 10

Elizabeth I 12

Mary, Queen of Scots 14

The Queen's Men 16

Poor Choices 18

FLASH POINT

   Act of Supremacy 20

   Mary and Darnley 22

   Rival Next Door 26

   Northern Rebellion 28

   Plotting Treason...................................... 30

   Mary's Fate 34

Golden Reign 36

Death of a Queen 38

Aftermath 40

Judgment 42

Timeline 44

Glossary 46

For Further Information 47

Index 48

AT ODDS

Queen Elizabeth I (1533–1603) reigned England for 45 years. Her reign was a period of stability and growth for England. Yet she had never expected to become queen.

* Unusually for a woman in 16th-century England, Elizabeth did not marry. She said that she was married to England.

* She restored England to the Protestant faith but was also tolerant of other religions.

* Elizabeth reportedly had no hair or eyebrows, but artists portrayed her as a powerful, attractive woman.

Mary, Queen of Scots (1542–1587), became the queen of Scotland when she was less than a week old. She also believed from a young age that she was the rightful heir to the English throne.

* Mary married three times. Her first marriage made her Queen of France.

* Mary was a Catholic. She wanted Scotland to reject Protestantism and return to Catholicism.

* Mary had a son with her second husband, Lord Darnley. He became King James VI of Scotland and later King James I of England.

* She was known for her great beauty.

* Mary spoke French because she was raised in France and her mother was French.

CONTEXT

Elizabeth I and Mary, Queen of Scots, were cousins. They were powerful women in a world that favored men. They both believed they had the right to the English throne.

Relations between England and its northern neighbor, Scotland, had been strained for centuries. In an effort to repair them, King Henry VII (1457–1509) married his daughter Margaret Tudor to James IV of Scotland in 1503. With the "Rose and Thistle" (England and Scotland) now united through marriage, it was hoped that the neighbors would coexist peacefully.

HOME: King Henry VIII spent much of his time at his new palace at Hampton Court.

PARENTS: Mary's parents were the Scottish king, James V, and his French wife, Mary of Guise.

Unhappy Kings

In 1509, Henry VII died and the throne passed to his son, King Henry VIII. The new king was anxious to have a male heir himself. His Spanish wife, Catherine of Aragon, gave birth to a son but the baby died. Finally, in 1516, she gave birth to a daughter, Mary. Without a male heir, Henry VIII wanted to marry a new wife. However, the Catholic religion stated that marriage only ended with the death of one of the partners. If Henry wanted to divorce Catherine, he would have to split

> " All the prelates at their consecration make an oath to the Pope clean contrary to the oath that they make to us, so that they seem to be his subjects, and not ours. "

King Henry VII, talking about Catholic priests

from the Roman Catholic church and its spiritual ruler, the Pope.

In Scotland, meanwhile, Henry VIII's nephew, King James V, and his wife, Mary of Guise, had two infant sons who died in 1541. Mary had a daughter, also named Mary, on December 8, 1542. Less than a week later, the king died and the baby became queen of Scotland.

The King's "Great Matter"

Henry VIII spent years working out how to rid himself of Catherine of Aragon. He decided that God had punished him with the lack of a son because Catherine was the widow of his elder brother and,

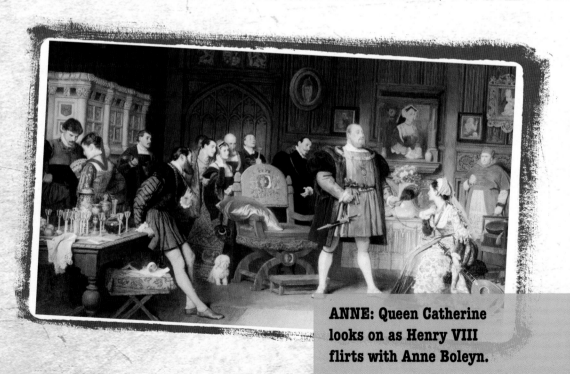

ANNE: Queen Catherine looks on as Henry VIII flirts with Anne Boleyn.

BOY: Edward VI came to the throne at the age of nine, but died when he was only fifteen.

as such, the two should never have married. Henry asked the Protestant Archbishop of Canterbury to grant him a divorce. Then he married Anne Boleyn in London on January 25, 1533. Their daughter Elizabeth was born on September 7 that same year. To help make the marriage legitimate, the Act of Supremacy (1534) made Henry head of the new Protestant Church of England. He disinherited Mary, his daughter by Catherine, and Elizabeth temporarily became his heir.

A Complicated Situation

Henry VIII later had four more wives. His third wife, Jane Seymour, finally produced a male heir, Edward. With Edward's birth, Elizabeth was no longer the heir to the throne. Edward became King Edward VI in 1547 but died six years later, aged just fifteen. Elizabeth's half-sister, Mary, became Queen Mary I. Under Mary, who is sometimes known as Mary Tudor, England became a Catholic country once more.

LINES ARE DRAWN

Two deaths made a clash between the cousins Princess Elizabeth and Mary, Queen of Scots inevitable and unavoidable.

After Edward VI's unexpected early death in 1553, his half-sister Mary Tudor became queen after the very brief nine-day reign of a rival claimant, Lady Jane Grey. Mary Tudor's reign was harsh and bloody. She was determined to return England to the Roman Catholic Church and she was willing to put to death anybody, even children, she suspected of still practicing the Protestant faith. Known as "Bloody Mary" she was a highly unpopular ruler. Her death in 1558 was greeted with widespread celebrations across England.

EXECUTION: Mary Tudor had so many Protestants executed she was nicknamed "Bloody Mary."

RETURN: Mary, Queen of Scots returns to Edinburgh after the death of King Francis II.

Death in France

Meanwhile, Mary, Queen of Scots, had been betrothed to Francis, the heir to the French crown, since the age of four and had been raised in France. She married him in April 1558. The next year, he became King Francis II of France, uniting the French and Scottish crowns. However, Francis died unexpectedly in 1560. The French crown passed to Francis's younger brother.

> **This quarrel now begun, is undoubtedly like to be a perpetual incumbrance of this kingdom.**
>
> **Sir William Cecil**

At 18 years old, Mary was a widow. She returned to Scotland to a Protestant country she barely knew. She had left when she was six and had been raised as a Catholic. She was still Queen of Scots, but now she wanted also to be Queen of England.

ELIZABETH I

Born to Henry VIII's second wife, Anne Boleyn, Elizabeth was brought up in obscurity. She did not expect to become queen.

On the death of her father, King Henry, in 1547, Elizabeth was the third in line to the throne. Henry had ordered the execution of Elizabeth's mother, Anne Boleyn, in 1536, when Elizabeth was just three years old, and had little to do with his daughter. Elizabeth had been briefly disinherited and her title had been lowered from "princess" to "lady". It was not until Henry married his sixth and last wife, Catherine Parr, that the queen brought Elizabeth into her

TOWER: Mary Tudor imprisoned Princess Elizabeth in the Tower of London.

> **" I will be as good unto ye as ever a Queen was unto her people. No will in me can lack, neither do I trust shall there lack any power. "**

Elizabeth on the eve of her coronation

CORONATION: Elizabeth was crowned queen of England on January 15, 1559.

household. Elizabeth was now given an education suitable for girls of the time. Despite Henry's lack of interest in his daughter, Elizabeth was extremely devoted to her father. She was very proud of his accomplishments as king.

An Uncertain Future

After the brief reigns of Edward VI and Lady Jane Grey, Elizabeth's Catholic half-sister Mary Tudor became Queen Mary I in July 1553. For a year, she had Elizabeth imprisoned because she believed Elizabeth supported Protestant rebels. Elizabeth had to learn the political skills to survive in a dangerous time. When it became clear that Mary was unlikely to have an heir, Elizabeth became heir apparent. Upon Mary Tudor's death on November 17, 1558, Elizabeth became queen.

MARY, QUEEN OF SCOTS

From her earliest childhood, Mary was a queen. For a brief period during her first marriage, she was queen of both Scotland and France.

CATHOLIC: Mary was raised a Catholic and remained dedicated to her faith.

Mary was raised a Catholic by her French mother, Mary of Guise, who brought her daughter up to expect great things. Henry VIII attempted to betroth his young son Edward to Mary when she was very young. The Scots nobles refused him. Instead, they betrothed Mary to Francis, the heir to the French throne.

A French Upbringing

At age five, Mary was sent to France to keep her safe from enemies in Scotland. She was raised at the court of Henry II. She stayed in France for the next thirteen years, spoke French, and was a favorite at court with everyone except her future mother-in-law, Henry II's queen, Catherine de' Medici. A noted beauty, Mary was smart and well educated.

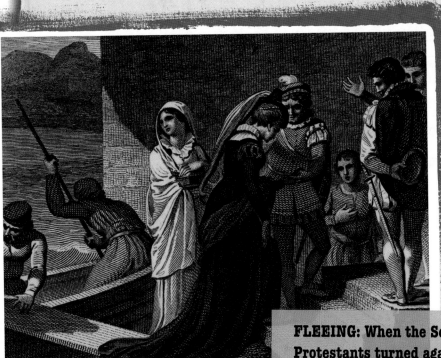

FLEEING: When the Scottish Protestants turned against Mary in 1567, she fled to England.

A Young Widow

With the death of her young husband, Francis, Mary had no choice but to return to Scotland. When she arrived back on August 19, 1561, nine months after her husband's death, she was shocked by her homeland. After France, Scotland seemed cold and backward. Worse still, it was controlled not by Catholics, but by Protestants with whom she would clearly clash.

> " I am their Queen and so they call me, but they use me not so. They must be taught to know their duties. "

Queen Mary talking about her Scottish subjects

THE QUEEN'S MEN

>> SKILLED ADVISORS

One reason Queen Elizabeth's reign was so long and successful was that she chose her closest advisors with the greatest of care.

Most women in Tudor England had little power or authority. Elizabeth was determined to prove that being a woman was no obstacle to ruling England. This meant never marrying, so no man could tell her what to do. Instead, she relied on their advice.

Elizabeth's State Officials

Elizabeth relied heavily on Sir William Cecil, 1st Baron Burghley, from the start of her reign until his death in 1598. Elizabeth appointed him secretary of state. He kept a tight control on the crown's finances making England a prosperous country.

COURTIERS: Elizabeth surrounded herself with loyal courtiers to advise her.

COUNCIL: Among Elizabeth's advisors were the Privy Council, a group of senior members of Parliament.

Another important advisor was Sir Francis Walsingham, who ran a network of spies and informers. It was his scheming that finally convicted Mary of plotting to kill her cousin Elizabeth. However, Cecil and Elizabeth's other advisors were alarmed by the Queen's close relationship with Robert Dudley, 1st Earl of Leicester. They feared she might marry him and that he would influence her to make poor decisions.

> **" You are like my little dog; when people see you, they know I am nearby. "**
>
> **Elizabeth I to Robert Dudley**

In the end, Elizabeth decided to remain married to her job. She suggested that Dudley should marry Mary, Queen of Scots, so that she could control Mary, but Dudley refused.

POOR CHOICES

Unlike Elizabeth, Mary did not make wise choices for either her close advisors or her husbands after the death of the King of France.

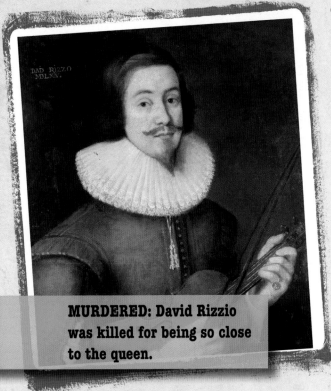

MURDERED: David Rizzio was killed for being so close to the queen.

On her return to Scotland in 1561, Mary sought out an unlikely advisor, her illegitimate half-brother James Stewart, 1st Earl of Moray. Lord James was the leader of the Protestants in Scotland and, despite their religious differences, Mary relied on his advice.

Ill-advised Advisors

Of the sixteen men in Mary's Privy Council, only four were Catholics. After Lord James, the advisor Mary most relied on was the Italian David Rizzio (also known as David Riccio). He became Mary's private secretary. By then Mary was married to her second husband, Lord Darnley. He was so jealous of Rizzio that in 1566 he joined a plot by Protestant nobles to murder the Italian. Darnley's involvement in Rizzio's murder may well have led to Darnley's own murder. He was found dead after an explosion in February 1567. Mary may have

BOTHWELL: The Earl of Bothwell was found not guilty of the murder of Darnley.

supported the plot to kill him. After Rizzio's murder, Mary relied for advice on James Hepburn, the fourth Earl of Bothwell. In 1567 Bothwell was tried for killing Darnley. He was found not guilty, but observers believed he intimidated the court to reach its verdict.

Bothwell and Mary married on May 15, 1567, dividing the loyalties of the country. The Scottish parliament imprisoned Mary and forced her to give up her throne to her son, James. Mary fled to England, hoping Elizabeth would help her.

> **She hath given over unto him her whole will, to be ruled and guided as himself best liketh.**

Thomas Randolph, English ambassador to Scotland, describes the marriage of Mary and Darnley

ACT OF SUPREMACY

One of Elizabeth's first acts as queen was to restore the Protestant faith. She became "supreme governor" of the Church of England.

The Supremacy Act was passed by Parliament in 1559. After the rule of the Catholic Mary I (Mary Tudor), the act reintroduced the anti-Catholic stand of Elizabeth's father, Henry VIII. From now on, anyone who wanted to hold public office in England had to swear an oath to the Queen, as head of the English or Anglican church, rather than to the Pope, who was head of the Roman Catholic Church. This meant all the key positions in the English government and church were held by Protestants. It also meant that Mary, Queen of Scots, could not become queen of England without first giving up her Catholic faith. Mary had already made it clear that her faith was of vital importance to her, however. She would never give it up.

OATH: The members of Parliament swear to uphold the Protestant faith.

Many Enemies

Despite the Supremacy Act, Elizabeth wanted to be a tolerant religious

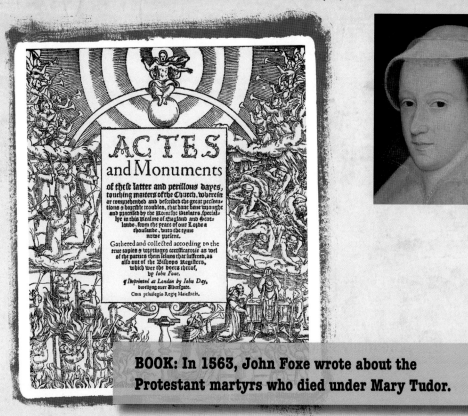

BOOK: In 1563, John Foxe wrote about the
Protestant martyrs who died under Mary Tudor.

leader. She generally treated English Catholics well, but that did not
stop her enemies, particularly the Roman Catholic Church, from
wanting her dead. In 1570, Pope Pius V excommunicated Elizabeth,
meaning that she was excluded from receiving the sacraments of the
Catholic Church and her subjects were released from their allegiance
to her as queen.

> **There is only
> one Christ, Jesus, one
> faith. All else is a
> dispute over trifles.**

**Queen Elizabeth comments on
religious differences**

In 1580, Pope Gregory XIII
proclaimed that anyone who
killed Elizabeth would not be
committing a sin. Both these
papal edicts increased Mary's
belief that she, as a loyal
Catholic, was the true queen
of England.

MARY AND DARNLEY

The two queens' opposing attitudes toward marriage underlined their different approaches toward the responsibility of being a ruler.

As long as Mary was married to the Dauphin (prince), later King Francis II of France, Elizabeth felt she did not need to worry about any plans her cousin might have for taking the English throne. However, when Mary was widowed in 1560 and made plain her intention to return to Scotland, Elizabeth realized she had a potentially serious problem to deal with.

Mary planned to marry to make a dynastic alliance. She knew that, as a queen, she was highly sought-after by many of the highest ranking European princes and kings. If Mary married into the royal families of Austria, Spain, or France, Elizabeth would end up with a powerful Catholic monarch on her doorstep.

SINGLE: Elizabeth I declared that she was married to England.

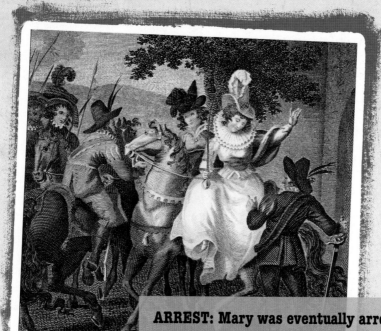

ARREST: Mary was eventually arrested by Scottish lords offended by the death of Darnley.

A Possible Match

Instead, Elizabeth wanted Mary to marry Elizabeth's childhood friend and favorite courtier, Robert Dudley. She planned to make the couple live with her, so that she could keep a close eye on Mary. In order to try to persuade Mary to accept Dudley, Elizabeth increased his social rank by making him the Earl of Leicester. But while Mary was in favor of the union, Dudley, who was widely believed to be in love with Elizabeth herself, refused to marry the Scottish queen.

> **At present it is not convenient; nor never shall be without some peril unto you and certain danger unto me.**

Elizabeth explains to Parliament why she will not marry, 1566

> **Destitute of a husband that by our self we were not able to sustain the pains and travail in our own person, it behoves us to yield unto one marriage or another.**

Mary writing to Elizabeth after she married Bothwell

FAVORITE: Elizabeth wanted Robert Dudley to marry Mary, but he refused.

Queen Elizabeth, meanwhile, had decided not to marry. She did not want to be in a position where she would have to obey her husband. The decision had far-reaching consequences. By choosing to remain the "virgin queen," Elizabeth would have no children. Her advisors despaired that the lack of an heir would bring uncertainty to the throne. They grew even more worried after Elizabeth was taken seriously ill with smallpox in October 1562. Mary wanted Elizabeth to proclaim her heir apparent, but Elizabeth refused to name any heir.

A Bad Marriage

In 1565 Mary decided to marry her cousin Henry Stewart, Lord Darnley, who was also a cousin of Elizabeth I. Mary's decision set the two queens on a collision course. Queen Elizabeth and her Privy

Council were against the Scottish queen marrying Darnley, whom they thought was too ambitious for power. In May 1565, the Privy Council sent a senior noble, Sir Nicholas Throckmorton, to Scotland to stop the marriage. He made the English case that the marriage would be "perilous to the amity between the queens and both realms." Throckmorton told Darnley to return to England and Mary promised the marriage would not take place. But on July 22, 1565, the marriage banns, or notices, were published. That meant the marriage would go ahead. Elizabeth was furious.

MESSENGER: Sir Nicholas Throckmorton failed to persuade Mary not to marry Darnley.

RIVAL NEXT DOOR

While Mary was living in France as queen, Elizabeth did not have to worry too much. But in 1561, Mary returned to Scotland.

A year after she had married Lord Darnley against Elizabeth's wishes, Mary, Queen of Scots, gave birth to their son, James. She now had a male heir. That same year, however, Mary fell out with her husband. Darnley became violently jealous of Mary's friendship with one of her courtiers, the Italian David Rizzio. Darnley plotted with other nobles to get rid of Rizzio. One evening when the Queen and Rizzio were eating, Darnley and his fellow plotters entered the room. They seized Rizzio, dragged him outside, and stabbed him to death.

THISTLE: Mary holds the Scottish national flower at her wedding to Darnley.

HOME: Rizzio was murdered in Mary's private apartments in Holyroodhouse Palace in Edinburgh.

Fleeing to England

A few months later, Darnley was killed after his cottage was blown up. It was rumored that the murder was arranged by the Earl of Bothwell, with Mary's approval. Tension grew between Elizabeth and Mary. When Mary married Bothwell soon after, the Scottish nobles also turned against her. They held her in a castle and forced her to make her infant son James king of Scotland in her place. In May 1568, Mary fled Scotland and begged for refuge from Elizabeth in England.

> **When you are acquitted of this crime, I will receive you with all honor; till this is done I may not.**

Elizabeth refuses to meet her cousin while Mary is suspected of Darnley's murder

NORTHERN REBELLION

Mary was a Catholic claimant to the English throne. Her presence in England encouraged Catholic subjects to rebel against Elizabeth.

Elizabeth and her cousin Mary wrote each other often—but they never met. Elizabeth kept Mary imprisoned in various castles and manor houses for nearly twenty years. Elizabeth feared that Mary's presence in England would encourage unrest. Old established families, such as the Catholic Norfolk family, resented the rise of Elizabeth's senior advisor, Sir William Cecil. Cecil was a Protestant and belonged to the new class that had benefitted when Henry VIII split from the Catholic Church. The Norfolks wanted to ruin Cecil. They planned to marry Mary to the fourth Duke of Norfolk.

CASTLE: Barnard Castle in County Durham was one of numerous places Mary was held.

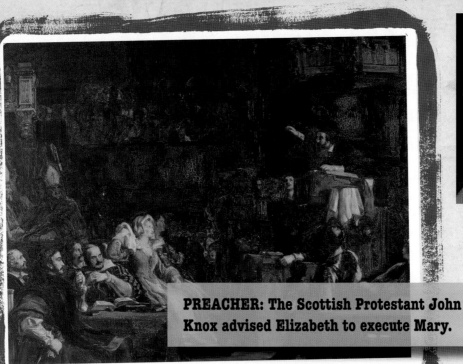

PREACHER: The Scottish Protestant John Knox advised Elizabeth to execute Mary.

The Northern Rebellion

When Elizabeth found out about the plot, she sent the Duke of Norfolk to the Tower of London. Encouraged by Mary's presence in England, powerful Catholic earls in the north led a rebellion against Elizabeth on November 9, 1569. It was not put down for four months.

It was a reminder of the threat posed by Mary's presence in England. Many of Elizabeth's advisors told her to execute Mary, but she was reluctant to execute a queen, so Mary remained imprisoned.

> " If you strike not at the root, the branches that appear to be broken will bud again with greater force. "

John Knox warns Elizabeth to take action against Mary, 1570

PLOTTING TREASON

Elizabeth's concern for her safety was not ill-placed. There were countless plots to murder her, many of which were inspired by Mary.

Since the papal edict of 1570 permitting the murder of Elizabeth, the queen's life had been in danger. There were many plots against her. Because Mary was a Catholic and because she continued to claim that she was the true queen of England, she was a figurehead for these plots. In fact, historians still debate how many plots Mary was aware of and how many were planned without her knowledge. The intelligence service run by Elizabeth's "spymaster," Sir Francis Walsingham, took 19 years to prove Mary's involvement in a plot.

ARREST: This portrait of Mary was painted during her long imprisonment.

SPYMASTER: Sir Francis Walsingham was in charge of ensuring Elizabeth's safety.

The Many Plots

In the 1570s and 1580s there were hundreds of plots to assassinate Elizabeth: none came close to succeeding. The best-known include the Ridolfi Plot of 1571. An Italian businessman named Roberto Ridolfi helped the Duke of Norfolk in a wild scheme to dethrone Elizabeth and bring Spanish troops to England. When the plot was discovered Norfolk was executed but Ridolfi escaped abroad.

In 1583, two significant plots against Elizabeth were uncovered: the

> **There are more than two hundred men of all ages who, at the instigation of the Jesuits, conspire to kill me.**
>
> Elizabeth I writes to the French ambassador, December 1563

Somerville Plot and the Throckmorton Plot. In October 1583, a Catholic named John Somerville planned to shoot Elizabeth with a pistol. He was arrested before he could carry out his plan and killed himself in his prison cell.

The next month, Walsingham's men arrested the Catholic Francis Throckmorton, who carried messages between Mary and the Spanish ambassador, Don Bernardino de Mendoza. Under torture, Throckmorton revealed that Mary's relation, the Duke of Guise, was planning to invade England. Throckmorton was executed and Mendoza sent back to Spain.

BEER: Anthony Babington smuggled letters to Mary in barrels.

CODE: This sheet of paper holds the key to the secret code Mary used for her letters.

The Babington Plot

Walsingham was desperate to give Queen Elizabeth concrete proof that Mary was involved in the many plots to kill her. He had his chance in 1586, when Anthony Babington and other English Catholics, encouraged by the new Spanish ambassador in London, plotted to kill Elizabeth. Babington and Mary wrote secret coded letters to one another. The letters were smuggled in beer barrels in and out of Chartley Hall in Derbyshire, where Mary was imprisoned.

Unknown to Mary or Babington, Walsingham's spies had infiltrated the plotters. Walsingham allowed the messages to continue in the hope that Mary would write something that proved she was involved in the plot. The plan worked: Mary's letters clearly showed that she knew about the plot to kill Elizabeth. This was the proof Walsingham needed to show the Queen.

MARY'S FATE

The discovery and proof that Mary was involved in the Babington Plot put Elizabeth in a very difficult position.

After the Babington Plot was uncovered, Mary was put on trial at Fotheringhay Castle in Northamptonshire. In October 1586, she was found guilty and sentenced to death. Elizabeth's advisors and Parliament wanted the death sentence to be carried out but

Elizabeth was unsure. Mary was not only her cousin. She was also Queen of Scotland. Elizabeth worried that killing a fellow monarch would set a terrible precedent.

A Death Warrant

Although Elizabeth had saved Mary from being accused of treason for years, she could no

TRIAL: Mary was tried by 36 nobles, including Elizabeth's closest advisors.

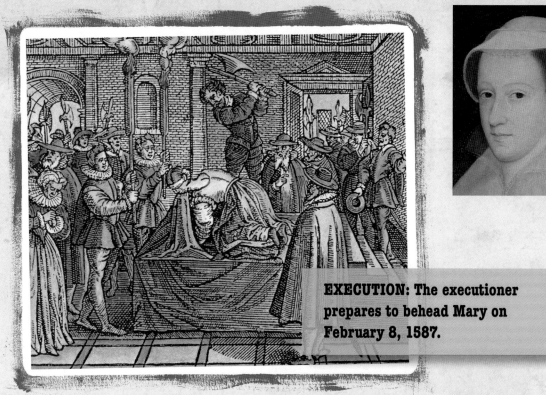

EXECUTION: The executioner prepares to behead Mary on February 8, 1587.

longer avoid the inevitable. But she was still reluctant to sign Mary's death warrant. Finally, on February 1, 1587, Elizabeth gave in and signed the warrant. She changed her mind at once, however, and did not send the warrant to Fotheringhay Castle. Sir William Cecil met the Privy Council secretly two days later, however, and decided the execution should go ahead. On February 8, 1587, Mary, Queen of Scots, was executed at Fotheringhay Castle, at age 44.

> **I protest I would not touch her. Neither hath my care been so much bent how to prolong mine as how to preserve both, which I am right sorry is made so impossible.**

Elizabeth to Sir William Cecil and others

GOLDEN REIGN

With Mary dead, Elizabeth devoted herself to England. Her greatest triumphs followed, starting with the defeat of Spain in 1588.

In the days following Mary's execution, Elizabeth was plunged into despair. Furious that the execution had taken place without her knowledge, Elizabeth banished her closest advisors, including Sir William Cecil himself. She also worried about how Scotland and France might react to the killing.

ENEMY: Philip II believed God would support his attempt to avenge the death of a Catholic monarch.

Good Queen Bess

As it turned out, it was not France or Scotland but Spain that provided the immediate threat. Elizabeth had believed that the execution of her cousin would spell the end of the Catholic threat to the English throne, but she was wrong. Philip II of Spain, the husband of Elizabeth's dead half-sister, Mary I (Mary Tudor), decided it was a good opportunity to overthrow Elizabeth and put a Catholic on the English throne.

ARMADA: The Spanish fleet was defeated by the English during severe weather in the English Channel.

Defeat of the Armada

Philip's 130-strong Armada, or war fleet, far outnumbered the English galleons. When the fleets clashed in the English Channel, however, poor Spanish leadership and bad weather led to a great English victory that marked the end of Spanish domination of the seas.

" I know I have the body of a weak and feeble woman, but I have the heart of a king, and a king of England too. "

Elizabeth addresses her troops on August 8, 1588, the day of the English victory

DEATH OF A QUEEN

Mary only learned that she was to be executed on the evening before her execution took place on February 8, 1587, at Fotheringhay Castle.

After her trial and conviction, Mary wrote many letters about her readiness to die for her faith. By dying as a Catholic martyr, Mary hoped that she could succeed where she had failed in life. Her death might raise Catholics from around Europe against Elizabeth. For her death, Mary wore black with a white veil on her head. But beneath her black dress was a red petticoat. Red was the color of martyrdom: it symbolized that Mary believed that she was dying for her faith.

TOMB: King James I built his mother a tomb in Westminster Abbey, near Elizabeth's tomb.

KING: James VI of Scotland became James I of England.

Scottish Reaction

While Mary's death angered the Scots, the Scottish parliament had sided with Elizabeth and did nothing to avenge her death. Mary's son, James VI of Scotland, was by now 21 years old. He was ambitious and eager to inherit the English throne on Elizabeth's death. He had spent no time with his mother.

Although he sent one of his nobles to plead for his mother's life, the Scottish king did not seem greatly moved by her death.

> " In my End is my Beginning. "

A quote embroidered by Mary during her imprisonment.

AFTERMATH

After Elizabeth recovered from the emotional crisis caused by Mary's death, her reign entered a golden era.

LONDON: Elizabeth's capital city was one of the most prosperous cities in the world.

The Elizabethan Age was a remarkable time in English history. Elizabeth's refusal to continue Queen Mary I's religious intolerance and her victory over Spain led to a great cultural flowering.

Until Elizabeth's death in 1603, England was at peace. During the last years of her reign, England became a wealthy country. Money flowed from the country's new colonies in the Americas, and there were no expensive wars with European rivals. Elizabeth encouraged the arts: poetry, theater, music and painting flourished. William Shakespeare wrote many of his greatest plays.

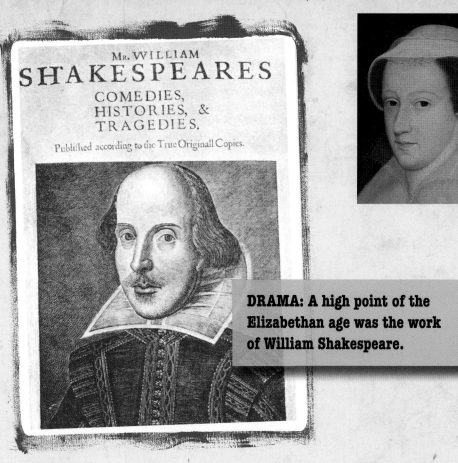

DRAMA: A high point of the Elizabethan age was the work of William Shakespeare.

United Country

Scotland lacked England's wealth, but it did have an ambitious king, James VI. He was determined to be named heir to the English throne, despite a 1585 law that barred relations of anyone who had plotted against Elizabeth from becoming monarch. Only in the month of Elizabeth's death in March 1603 did the English confirm that James would inherit the throne. He was crowned King James I of England on July 25, 1603, bringing England and Scotland together under his rule.

> " Kings are justly called gods for they exercise a manner or resemblance of divine power upon earth. "
>
> **King James VI and I**

JUDGMENT

ELIZABETH I OF ENGLAND Vs. MARY, QUEEN OF SCOTS

Elizabeth I's reputation remains high. She ruled over a period of great artistic and economic achievement in England. However, she had done nothing to secure the future of the Tudor dynasty.

* Elizabeth's refusal to marry meant that she would die without an heir, bringing instability to the throne.

* Elizabeth refused a request from Mary, Queen of Scots, to make Mary heir apparent.

* Elizabeth did not really know how to deal with Mary, so she imprisoned her for many years.

* Elizabeth knew Mary was a focus for plots against her, but she was reluctant to execute someone who was also a monarch.

Mary, Queen of Scots, is sometimes seen as having caused her own downfall. However, she was dedicated to her Catholic faith, and believed she had little choice about her actions.

* Mary chose her associates badly. Her marriage to the ambitious Earl of Bothwell turned the Scottish nobles against her.

* In England, Mary kept repeating her claim to the throne. That put her cousin Elizabeth in a difficult position.

* Mary took a risk by becoming involved in at least one plot against Elizabeth.

* Mary's faith was so important to her that she seized her chance to become a martyr.

TIMELINE

Although Queen Elizabeth and Mary, Queen of Scots never met, they each had a profound influence on the other's life, particularly after the death of Mary's first husband in 1561.

Infant Queen
On the death of her father, King James V, Mary becomes queen of Scotland when she is still less than a week old.

Return to Scotland
On the death of her first husband, King Francis II of France, Mary returns home to Scotland after spending over a decade in France.

Second Marriage
After Darnley is killed, Mary marries the noble who is tried for the murder, Lord Bothwell. The marriage infuriates powerful Scottish Protestants.

1542 **1558** **1561** **1565** **1567**

Elizabethan Age
Elizabeth I of England comes to the throne in November after the death of her sister, Mary I (Mary Tudor).

A Poor Marriage
In July, Mary marries Henry, Lord Darnley, who is a cousin of both Mary and Elizabeth. They have a son, James.

Forced Abdication
Scottish nobles imprison Mary and force her to abdicate on July 24 in favor of her son, who becomes James VI of Scotland.

Escape to England
Fearing for her life, Mary escapes from Scotland and flees to England, where Elizabeth puts her under house arrest in various castles for the next 19 years.

Catholic Rebellion
Encouraged by Mary's presence in England, the Catholic earls of Northumberland and Westmoreland begin the Northern Rebellion against Elizabeth; it lasts only four months.

Death of the Queen
On February 8, Mary is beheaded in Fotheringhay Castle after the Privy Council order her execution to go ahead without the knowledge of Queen Elizabeth.

1568 **1569** **1586** **1587** **1603**

The Queen's Support
Elizabeth makes representations to the Scots that Mary should be restored to the Scottish throne, but the Scots reject the idea.

Babington Plot
Secret letters are discovered that show Mary to be aware of a Catholic plot to kill Elizabeth. Mary is arrested, tried, and found guilty of treason.

A Scottish King
When Elizabeth dies on March 24, Mary's son James VI of Scotland also becomes King James I of England, finally uniting the two countries under his rule.

GLOSSARY

Anglican Relating to the Church of England established by Henry VIII.

assassinate To kill someone for political or ideological reasons.

banns Notices that must be read out in church ahead of time before a wedding can take place.

betroth To formally promise that someone will marry someone else.

colonies Foreign territories governed by a different country.

courtier Someone who attends a royal court as a companion or advisor to the monarch.

disinherited Removed a beneficiary from a will.

edicts Official announcements made by people with authority.

excommunicated Excluded from taking part in any services of the Catholic Church.

heir Someone who will inherit a position on the death or retirement of its current occupant.

heir apparent An heir whose inheritance cannot be changed, even by the birth of another heir.

illegitimate Someone who is born to parents who are not married.

legitimate Describes someone who is legally entitled to their position.

martyr Someone who is killed for their political or religious beliefs.

plot A secret plan by a group of people to do something illegal.

precedent An event or action that sets an example that can be followed in the future.

prelates Bishops or other senior church figures.

Privy Council A group of senior members of Parliament who advised the monarch on important decisions.

Protestantism A branch of Christianity that was formed in the early 16th century as a protest against the practices of the Catholic Church.

sacraments Church ceremonies that are thought to give the participants increased spiritual grace.

spymaster Someone who is in charge of gathering information through secret means.

treason The crime of trying to overthrow a monarch or government.

warrant A legal document that authorizes officials to arrest someone or to carry out the sentence of a court.

FOR FURTHER INFORMATION

Books

Hilliam, Paul. *Elizabeth I: Queen of England's Golden Age* (Rulers, Scholars, and Artists of the Renaissance). Rosen Publishing Group, 2004.

Hinds, Kathryn. *Elizabeth and her Court* (Life in Elizabethan England). Cavendish Square Publishing, 2007.

Lotz, Nancy, and Carlene Phillips. *Mary, Queen of Scots* (European Queens). Morgan Reynolds Publishing, 2007.

MacDonald, Fiona. *You Wouldn't Want to be Mary, Queen of Scots!* Children's Press, 2008.

Weatherly, Myra. *Elizabeth I: Queen of Tudor England* (Signature Lives: Renaissance Era). Compass Point Books, 2005.

Websites

http://www.bbc.co.uk/history/people/mary_queen_of_scots/
BBC website about the life of Mary, Queen of Scots, with links to videos from BBC documentaries.

http://www.historylearningsite.co.uk/mary_queen_of_scots.htm
History Learning Site pages about Mary, Queen of Scots.

http://www.history.com/topics/british-history/elizabeth-i
History.com page about Elizabeth I, with links to other pages.

http://www.historyonthenet.com/tudors/elizabeth_mary_queen_of_scots.htm
A page from History on the Net about the rivalry between Elizabeth and Mary.

http://www.npg.org.uk/collections/search/person/mp01452/queen-elizabeth-i
A site from the National Portrait Gallery in London with many different portraits of Queen Elizabeth I.

INDEX

Act of Supremacy 9, 20–21
Archbishop of Canterbury 9
Armada, Spanish 37

Babington Plot 33, 34–35
Barnard Castle 28
Boleyn, Anne 9, 12
Bothwell, Earl of 19, 24, 27, 43

Catherine of Aragon 7, 8
Catholicism 5, 8, 10, 14, 20,
    28, 30, 36, 38
Cecil, Sir William 11, 16, 28,
    35, 36
Chartley Hall 33
Church of England 9, 20–21
colonies 40

Darnley, Lord 5, 18, 24–25,
    26, 27
divorce, Henry VII 7
Dudley, Robert 17, 23

Edinburgh 27
Edward VI, king of England 9,
    10, 13
Elizabethan Age 40–41
execution, of Mary, Queen of
    Scots 35, 38

Fotheringhay Castle 34, 35, 38
Foxe, John 21
France 5, 14, 36
Francis II, king of France 11, 14,
    15, 22

Gregory XIII, Pope 21
Grey, Lady Jane 10, 13
Guise, Duke of 32

Hampton Court 6
heir, to the English throne
    24, 42
Henry II, king of France 14
Henry VII, king of England 6,
    7, 20
Henry VIII, king of England 6,
    7, 8, 12, 13, 14, 28
Hepburn, James see Bothwell,
    Earl of

James 27
James IV, king of Scotland 6
James V, king of Scotland 7, 8
James VI, king of Scotland
    (James I of England) 15, 27,
    39, 41

Knox, John 29

London, Elizabethan 40

marriage, of Mary 22, 23, 24
marriage, of Elizabeth 4
martyrdom 21, 38, 43
Mary I, Queen 7, 9, 10, 13
Mary of Guise 7, 8, 14
Mary Tudor see Mary I
Mendoza, Bernardino de 32

Norfolk, Duke of 31
Norfolk family 28, 29
Northern Rebellion 28–29

papacy 8, 20
papal edict 30
Parr, Catherine 12
Philip II, King of Spain 36
Pius V, Pope 21

plots, against Elizabeth
    30–33, 42
Privy Council 17, 18, 25, 35
Protestantism 4, 9, 13, 18, 20

Randolph, Thomas 19
Riccio, David see Rizzio,
    David
Ridolfi Plot 31
Rizzio, David 18, 26

Scotland 6, 41
Seymour, Jane 9
Shakespeare, William 40, 41
Somerville Plot 32
Spain 32, 36
Stewart, Henry see Darnley,
    Lord
Stewart, James, Early of
    Moray 18

Throckmorton Plot 32
Throckmorton, Sir Nicholas
    25
timeline 44–45
Tower of London 12, 29

"virgin queen," image 24

Walsingham, Sir Francis 17, 30,
    31, 33, 34
women, in Elizabethan life 16